Little Book of
BlokeJokes

CARLTON
BOOKS

First published in 2004 by Carlton Books Limited
An imprint of the Carlton Publishing Group
20 Mortimer Street
London W1T 3JW

Text © 2001 and 2003

A catalogue record for this book is available
from the British Library.

ISBN 13: 978-1-84442-704-8
ISBN 10: 1-84442-704-8

Printed and bound in Singapore

10 9 8 7 6 5

Why do **blokes** get **married?**

So they don't have to hold their stomachs in anymore.

Why did the **bloke** put **Viagra** in his eyes?

He wanted to look hard.

Why do **women** need **blokes**?

Because vibrators can't get a round of drinks in.

Why do **blokes** like **smart women**?

Opposites attract.

Why do **blokes** keep empty milk bottles in the fridge?

In case anyone wants their coffee black.

Why do **blokes** have **legs**?

So their brains don't drag on the floor.

Why do **blokes** whistle
when they're **sitting**
on the **toilet**?

So they can remember which
end to wipe.

Why is **Santa** such a **happy bloke**?

Because he knows where all the bad girls live.

Why do **blokes** want to **marry virgins**?

Because they can't stand criticism.

Why can't **blokes** make **ice cubes**?

They don't know the recipe.

Why do **blokes** propose?

Because they can't afford
our wages!

Why do **little boys** whine?

Because they're practising to be blokes.

Why was **Colonel Sanders** a **typical bloke**?

All he cared about were legs, breasts and thighs.

Why do **blokes** need
instant replay on
TV sports?

Because after 30 seconds they
forget what happened.

Why are **bankers** good lovers?

They know the penalty for early withdrawals.

Why did the **bloke** cross the **road**?

God knows, why do they bother doing anything?

Why did the **bloke** ask all his **friends** to **save** their **burnt-out** light bulbs?

Because he was trying to build a darkroom.

Why does a **penis** have a **hole** in the **end**?

So blokes can be open-minded.

Why does it **snow** at **Christmas**?

Because Santa's coming.

Why shouldn't you hit a **bloke** with **glasses**?

A baseball bat is much more effective.

Why did the **stupid bloke** get a **stabbing pain** in his **eye** every time he drank a **cup of tea**?

He forgot to take the spoon out.

Why should you **never** try to find a bloke's **inner child**?

Because you'll have enough trouble coping with his outer one.

Why were **blokes** given **larger brains** than **dogs**?

So they wouldn't hump women's legs at cocktail parties.

Why don't **single** women **fart?**

Because they don't get a bum till they're married.

Why are **women** more **intelligent** than blokes?

Because diamonds are a girl's best friend ... while man's best friend is a dog.

Why does it take **one million** sperm to **fertilise** just **one egg**?

Because they come from a bloke, so they won't stop to ask for directions.

Why did **God** put **blokes' sexual organs** on the **outside**?

So they remember where they are.

Why don't **women** have **blokes' brains**?

Because they don't have penises to keep them in.

? ?

Why do **men** like to make salads?

Because they're born tossers.

What do you give the **bloke** who has **everything**?

Penicillin.

What do you **never** want to **hear** while having **great sex**?

Honey, I'm home!

What do you call an **attractive, intelligent** and **sensitive man**?

A rumour.

What's the difference between a **man** and a **yoghurt**?

A yoghurt has culture.

What's the **best revenge** when a **woman steals** your **bloke**?

Let her keep him.

What do you do with a **bloke** who thinks he's **God's gift** to women?

Take him back and exchange him.

What happens when a **woman** makes a **fool** of a **bloke**?

It's usually an improvement.

What's the difference between **Bigfoot** and an **intelligent bloke**?

Bigfoot's been spotted several times.

What's the **best place** to hide a **bloke's** birthday present?

The washing basket.

What's the difference between a **bloke** with a **mid-life crisis** and a **clown**?

A clown knows he's wearing funny clothes.

What's a **bloke's** idea of **foreplay**?

Prodding you to see if you're awake.

What can you say to a **bloke** who's just had **sex**?

Anything you like – he's asleep.

What's a **bloke's** definition of **conflict** of **interest**?

When pizza arrives during sex.

What's a **bloke's** idea of **helping** around the **house**?

Dropping his clothes where you can pick them up.

Ten Things **Blokes** Know About **Women**:

1.
2.
3.
4.
5.
6.
7.
8.
9.
10. They have tits.

A bloke says to God: 'God, why did you make woman so beautiful?'

God says: 'So you would love her.'

'But God,' the bloke says. 'Why did you make her so dumb?'

God says: **'So she would love you.'**

What would have happened if it had been **three Wise Women** instead of **three Wise Men**?

They would have asked for directions, arrived on time, helped deliver the baby, cleaned the stable, made a casserole and brought practical gifts.

Why do only
10 per cent of **blokes**
make it to **heaven**?

Because if they all went, it would
be hell.

Why did **God** create **alcohol**?

So ugly blokes would get the chance to have sex.

What's the **difference** between a **bloke** and a **Brussels sprout**?

One is tasteless and smells of farts and the other is a nutritious vegetable!

What's the **difference** between a **bloke** and a **vibrator**?

A vibrator won't make you sleep in the wet patch.

What's the **difference** between **blokes** and **women**?

A woman wants one bloke to satisfy her every need. A bloke wants every woman to satisfy his one need.

What's the **difference** between a **bloke** and **ET**?

ET phones home.

What's the difference between **blokes** and **women**?

Women dream of world peace, a safe environment and eliminating hunger. Blokes dream of being stuck in a lift with Destiny's Child.

What's the **difference** between a **single bloke** and a **married bloke**?

A single bloke will lie awake all night thinking about something you say. A married bloke will fall asleep before you finish.

What's the **difference** between a **bloke** and a **bird**?

A bird can whistle through its pecker.

What's the difference between **blokes' sex talk** and **women's sex talk**?

When a bloke talks dirty to a woman, it's sexual harassment. When a woman talks dirty to a bloke, it's 49p a minute.

What's the **difference** between a **bloke** and a **catfish**?

One's a bottom-feeding scum-sucker – the other's a fish!

A **bloke's** sitting in a **cinema,** and when the **usherette** asks to see his **ticket**, he **flashes** at her.

Unfazed, she says:'I asked to see your ticket - not your stub!'!

How do **blokes** sort their **laundry**?

'Filthy' and 'filthy, but wearable'.

How does a **bloke** keep his **youth**?

By giving her money, diamonds and designer clothes.

How many **blokes** does it take to **change** a **light bulb**?

Two – one to change the bulb and one to collect the medal.

How do you **stop** a **bloke biting** his **nails**?

Make him wear shoes.

How many **blokes** does it take to put the **toilet seat** down?

Nobody knows.
It hasn't happened yet.

How do you **stop** a **bloke** breaking into your **house**?

Replace all the locks with bra fasteners.

How do you get a **bloke** to **climb** up on the **roof**?

You tell him the drinks are on the house.

How do you **confuse a bloke**?

You don't, they're just born that way.

How many **blokes** does it take to **change** a **light bulb**?

Three – one to screw in the bulb, and two to listen to him brag about the screwing part.

How do you **start** a **conversation** with a **bloke** in a **flower shop**?

'So, what did you do?'

How do you stop **blokes** from **spitting**?

Turn down the grill.

How do you **reply** to a **bloke** who says: **'I knew that!** I'm not a complete **idiot**, you know!'

'Oh! What part is missing then?'

How do you **kill** a **bloke**?

Ask him to jump off his ego and land on his IQ.

How many **blokes** does it take to **change** a **light bulb**?

As many as you like – it'll still be there waiting to be changed in the morning.

How do you stop your **bloke** reading your **email**?

Rename the mail folder 'instruction manuals'.

How do you **spot** the most **popular bloke** at the **nudist colony**?

He's the one who can have a cup of coffee in each hand and still carry a dozen doughnuts.

How do you **know** when a **bloke's** had an **orgasm**?

He snores.

How do you **make** a **bloke** scream when you are having **sex**?

Phone him.

How many **men** does it take to **change** a **light bulb**?

None, they just sit there in the dark and complain.

How do we know **blokes** invented **maps**?

Who else would turn an inch into a mile?

How can you **spot** a **blind bloke** at a **nudist colony**?

It isn't hard.

How many **men** does it take to **change** a **light bulb**?

None. They're happy living in the shadows.

How many **bloke** jokes are there?

None, they're all true.

How do you make **7 pounds** of **fat** look attractive to a **bloke**?

Put a nipple on it.

How do most **blokes define marriage**?

A very expensive way of getting their laundry done for free.

How do you make a **bloke's** eyes **light up**?

Shine a torch in his ear.

How does a **man** show
that he is **planning** for
the **future**?

He buys two cases of beer.

How is being at a **singles bar** different to being at the **circus**?

At the circus, the clowns don't talk.

How do **blokes'** brain cells die?

Alone.

How do you know when it's time to **wash dishes** and **clean** the **house**?

Look inside your pants; if you have a penis, it's not time.

How do you **scare blokes**?

Sneak up behind them and start throwing confetti.

How do you know a **bloke** wants **sex**?

He's awake.

How do **blokes** practise **safe sex**?

They meet their mistresses at least 50 miles from home.

How can you make sure your **bloke** doesn't make a **fool** of himself at a **party**?

Leave him at home.

How can you tell that **women** have a **sense** of **humour**?

They get married.

A **bloke** goes to see a **psychiatrist** wearing only **clingfilm** for shorts.

The shrink says:
'Well, I can clearly see you're nuts.'

A **bloke** goes to the **doctor's** with a **flywheel** **between** his **legs**. The **doctor** asks: 'What's that?' And the **bloke** replies: 'I don't know, but it's **driving** me **nuts**!'

A **bloke** goes to the **doctor** with a piece of lettuce sticking out of his bum. He tells the doctor he's a little **concerned,** and asks for an examination.

After a little **probing,** the doctor turns to his patient and says, 'It's **worse** than I originally thought – that's just the **tip** of the **iceberg**.'

A **bloke** goes to the **doctor** and says: 'Doctor, every time I **sneeze**, I have an **orgasm**.' The doctor says: 'What are you **taking** for it?' And the bloke replies: '**Pepper**!'

Why are **blokes** like **old bras**?

They hang around your boobs all day and give you no support when it's needed.

Why are **blokes** like **photocopiers**?

You need them for reproduction, but that's about it.

Why are **blokes** like **textbooks**?

You have to spend a lot of time between the covers to gain a small amount of satisfaction.

Why are **blokes** like **crystal**?

Some look really good, but you can still see right through them.

Why are **blokes** like **lawnmowers**?

They're hard to get started, they emit noxious odours and half the time they don't work.

Why are **blokes** like **fine wine**?

They all start out like grapes, and it's our job to stomp on them and keep them in the dark until they mature into something you'd like to have dinner with.

Why are **blokes** like **newborn** babies?

They're cute at first, but pretty soon you get tired of cleaning up their crap.

Why are **blokes** like curling **tongs**?

They're always hot and in your hair.

Why are **blokes** like **adverts**?

You can't believe a word they say.

Why are **blokes** like **miniskirts**?

If you're not careful, they'll creep up your legs.

Why are **blokes** like microwave **meals**?

They're both finished in 30 seconds.

Why are **blokes** like **bananas**?

The older they get, the less firm they are.

Why are **sensitive blokes** like **UFOs**?

You often hear about them, but you never see one.

Why are **blokes** like the **weather**?

You can't do anything to change either of them.

Why are **blokes** like **government bonds**?

Because they take so long to mature.

Why are **blokes** like **tights**?

They either cling, run or don't fit right in the crotch!

Why are **blokes** like **dogs**?

They're smelly, constantly demand food and are both afraid of vacuum cleaners.

Two **aliens** are circling Earth, discussing its **inhabitants**. 'So what do you think? **Intelligent life** or not?' asks the first alien.

And the second answers: 'Hmm, the ones with the **brains** seem to be OK, but I'm not so sure about the ones with the **balls**!'

A **fat bloke** sees a notice in a shop window: 'A **bed**, a **woman** and a **pie** for £5.' He goes into the shop and says to the owner: 'Is that right – a bed, a woman and a pie for only £5?'

'Of course,' says the shopkeeper. 'Sounds like a bargain, but what kind of pies are they?' asks the fat bloke.

This **bloke** walks into a bar and says: **'OUCH!** Who put that there?'

A bloke goes before a judge to try to get excused from jury service, and the judge asks him why he can't serve as a juror. 'I don't want to be away from my job for that long,' replies the bloke. 'Can't they do without you at work?' asks the judge. **'Yes,' says the bloke. 'But I don't want them to know it.'**

What's a **bloke's** idea of
honesty in a relationship?

Telling you his real name.

What's a **bloke's** idea of **foreplay**?

Watching the end of the match first.

What do **blokes** use for **birth** control?

Their personalities.

What do you call that **insensitive** bit at the **base** of the **penis**?

A bloke.

What's the **fastest** way to a **bloke's** heart?

Through his chest with a sharp implement.

What do you call a **bloke** who says he's in **touch** with his **feminine** side?

A liar!

What should you give a **bloke** who has **everything**?

A woman to show him how to work it.

What's the **best** way to **kill a bloke**?

Put a naked woman and a six-pack in front of him. Then tell him to pick just one.

What do you **say** to a **bloke** if he asks you whether you **fancy** a **quickie**?

'As opposed to what?'

What do you call a **bloke** with a **small willy**?

Justin …

What do **single blokes** have if mums have **Mother's Day** and dads have **Father's Day**?

Palm Sunday.

What's the **definition** of **mixed emotions**?

Watching the bloke who just dumped you crash into your spanking new car.

What should you do with your **bum** before having **sex**?

Drop him off at the golf club.

What **happens** when a **vain** and **irritating** bloke takes **Viagra**?

He gets taller.

What do you call a **man** who does the **washing up**, cleaning and is always **polite** and **helpful**?

A wo-man.

What do you call a **bloke** with a **big willy** and **lots of cash**?

Darling.

What is **six-inches** long, **three-inches** wide and drives women **wild**?

A £50 note!

What do you call a **bloke** with an **IQ** of **five**?

Gifted.

What does it mean when a **bloke** is in your bed, **gasping** for **breath** and calling **your name**?

You didn't hold the pillow down long enough.

What do you call a **woman** with half a **brain cell**?

A bloke.

What do you call a **zit** on a **bloke's penis**?

A brain tumour.

What do you call a **fly** in a **bloke's brain**?

Space invader.

What should you say to a **bloke** whose chat-up line is: 'Do you want to **come home** and **sit** on my **face**?'

'Why, is your nose bigger than your penis?'

What should you do if you see your **ex-boyfriend** rolling around **in pain** on the **ground**?

Shoot him again.

What did the **elephant** say to the **naked bloke**?

How do you drink with that?

What's more useful – a **bloke** or a **chocolate fireguard**?

Well, a chocolate fireguard can make a lovely sauce.

What's got **eight arms** and an **IQ** of **60**?

Four blokes watching a football game.

What do you call a **bunch of blokes** in a **circle**?

A dope ring.

What's the **definition** of a **male chauvinist pig**?

A bloke who hates every bone in a woman's body, except his own.

What's a **bloke's** idea of **romance**?

You go and fetch him another can after sex.

What makes blokes **chase women** they have **no** intention of **marrying**?

The same urge that makes dogs chase cars they have no intention of driving.

What's the **definition** of a **bloke**?

A vibrator with a wallet!

What did the **elephant** say to the **bloke**?

'It's cute, but can you pick up peanuts with it?!'

What's the **best** form of **birth control** for a **bloke** over 50?

Nudity.

A bloke steps on to one of those speak-your-weight machines that also tell your fortune. 'Listen to this,' he tells his wife, showing her a small white card. 'It says I'm energetic, bright, resourceful and a great lover.'

'Yes,' his wife nods. **'And it's got your weight wrong, too!'**

A boring bloke says to his wife: 'Honey, why are you wearing your wedding ring on the wrong finger?' **And the bored wife replies: 'Because I married the wrong man!'**

A bloke walks into the bedroom to find his wife jumping up and down on the bed. She says: 'I've just had my annual check-up and the doctor says I may be 45, but I've got the breasts of an 18 year old!' 'Yeah,' says the bloke. 'And what did he say about your 45-year-old arse?' **'Oh, he didn't mention you, dear.'**

An **obnoxious bloke** tries to **apologise** to a **female** colleague, saying: 'I'm **sorry** I put you in such an **awkward position** the other day.

Not feeling in a **forgiving mood**, she replies: 'There's not a position between one and 69 that I'd ever care to be in with you.'

If you have an **intelligent woman**, an **intelligent bloke** and **Santa Claus** in a lift, which one is the odd one out?

The intelligent woman – because the other two don't exist.

Did you hear about the **woman** who finally figured **blokes** out?

She died laughing before she could tell anybody.